W9-BMO-915

JOSEPH MIDTHUN SAMUEL HITI

SUBTRACTION

www.worldbook.com

World Book, Inc.
180 North LaSalle Street
Suite 900
Chicago, Illinois 60601
USA

For information about other World Book publications,
visit our website at www.worldbook.com
or call 1-800-WORLDBK (967-5325).
For information about sales to schools and libraries,
call 1-800-975-3250 (United States),
or 1-800-837-5365 (Canada).

Building Blocks of Mathematics:
Subtraction
ISBN: 978-0-7166-7897-7 (trade, hc.)
ISBN: 978-0-7166-1478-4 (pbk.)
ISBN: 978-0-7166-1876-8 (e-book, EPUB3)
ISBN: 978-0-7166-2446-2 (e-book, PDF)

Acknowledgments:
Created by Samuel Hiti and Joseph Midthun
Art by Samuel Hiti
Text by Joseph Midthun
Special thanks to Anita Wager,
Hala Ghousseini, and Syril McNally

TABLE OF CONTENTS

WHAT IS SUBTRACTION?

You know how to add up numbers, right?

I'm Subtraction!

Well, I look at things differently.

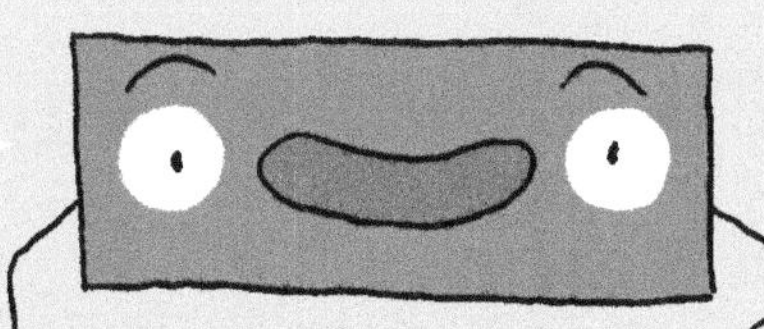

I help you find the difference between two amounts!

See this?

This is a subtraction problem!

If you have 3 and take away 2, what's the difference?

3-2=?

You could also write it like this:
squeak

Say you have 3 triangles and take away 2...
The difference is 1 triangle!
squeak
squeak

You can use me in all kinds of ways!
Come on. I'll show you!

How many peaches will you have if we take away the 7 rotten ones?

$16 - 7 = ?$

Let's work together to solve the problem. How should we start?
Well, I could count up the good ones...

True, but I've got another way to solve it.
Hmm.

15,
14,
13,
12,
11,
10,
9.
9 peaches are left over!
Hey-
I get it!
Squeak
squeak
squeak
squeak
squeak
squeak
squeak

You're counting back!
That's right!
I started at 16 and counted back 7.

You could also use me to solve 16 - 7.

How can addition help us solve a subtraction problem?

1 2, 3, 4, 5, 6, 7.

3 are left over. Don't forget to add the 6 ones back!

NUMBER LINES

Have you ever used a number line?

A number line can help you solve equations like this one:

$$37 - 19 = ?$$

Counting back on a number line is like taking away.

Let's use the number line to help us find the answer to 37 - 19!

Where do we start?

Let's start on 37.

Plop

37

Now we can count back to 19 to find the answer.

Cool!

37

First, let's jump back by 10!
Now what do we have?
27!
Let's jump back 10 more!
plop
19
27
37

Oops! We jumped back a total of 20.
plop
17
19
27

We only needed to jump back 19.
What should we do?
Let's add 1 back!

There's our answer!
18!
HOP
17
18
19

37 - 19 equals 18!
Let's make sure!

CHECKING YOUR WORK

You can always use addition to check an answer you found with subtraction.

plop

18

19

37

First, make a jump of 10!
29!
Let's add 1 to make it 30.
Plop
19
29
37

Now we can see 37!
How many jumps did we make?
Plop
29
30
31
32
33
34
35
36
37

Let's count them up!
10 + 1 + 7 =

18!
The same answer as before!
We should do this more often!

LOSING YOUR MARBLES

Nice shot!

Wow, you're pretty good at playing marbles!

Practice makes perfect!

WACK

FWIP

TUMP

I started with 53 marbles.

53

Then, I lost 25 over the course of the game.

25

Let's count back to figure out how many I have left.

Hold on!

Could we try regrouping the numbers first?

How?

Let's regroup 53 into tens and ones.

53 is the same as...

50 + 3

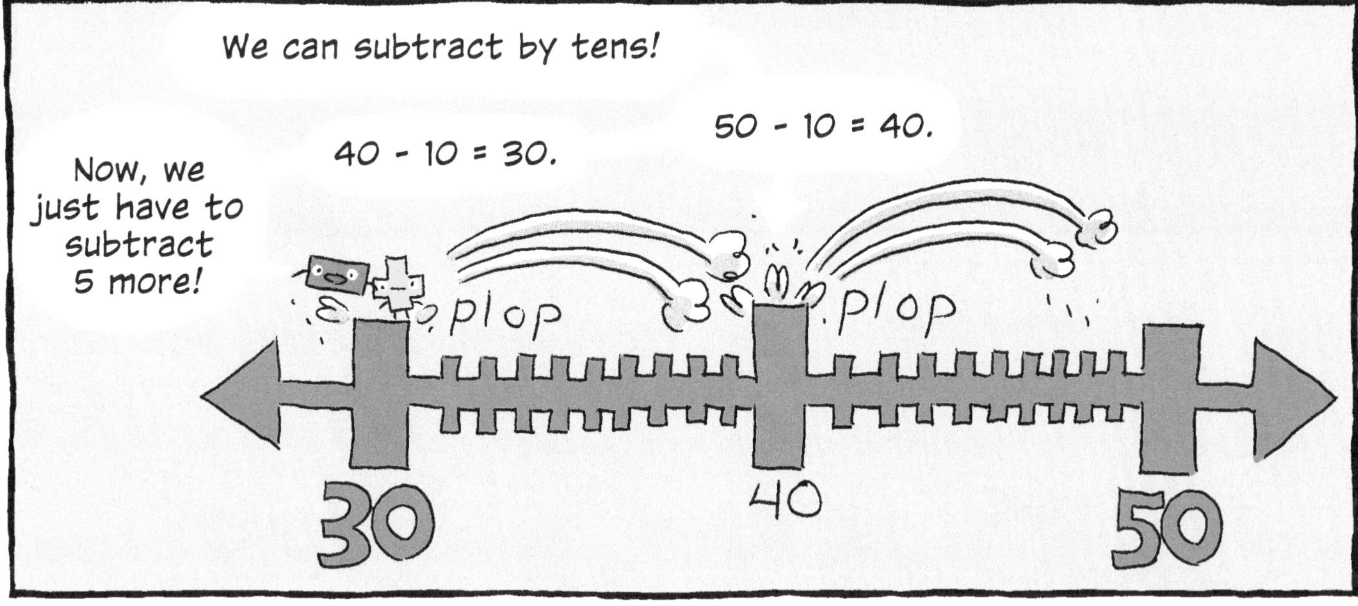

Is there a faster way to solve the same problem?

Why don't we try using doubles?

So, then...

50 − 25 = 25

Perfect!
However, we started with 53 marbles.

So we need to add 3 to our answer.

Like this!
25 3 =

28!
I haven't lost all my marbles!
28

Heh heh...
...not yet!

What was that?!
Oh, nothing.
Let's find more things to subtract!

I need some more bait!

whip

ZZZZ

PLOP

I only managed to catch 8 worms!

Sniff.
Sniff.
Don't sweat it!

Let's find out how many got away!
Um...
Plop

Let's look at it like this:
15 − ? = 8

FREEDOM!

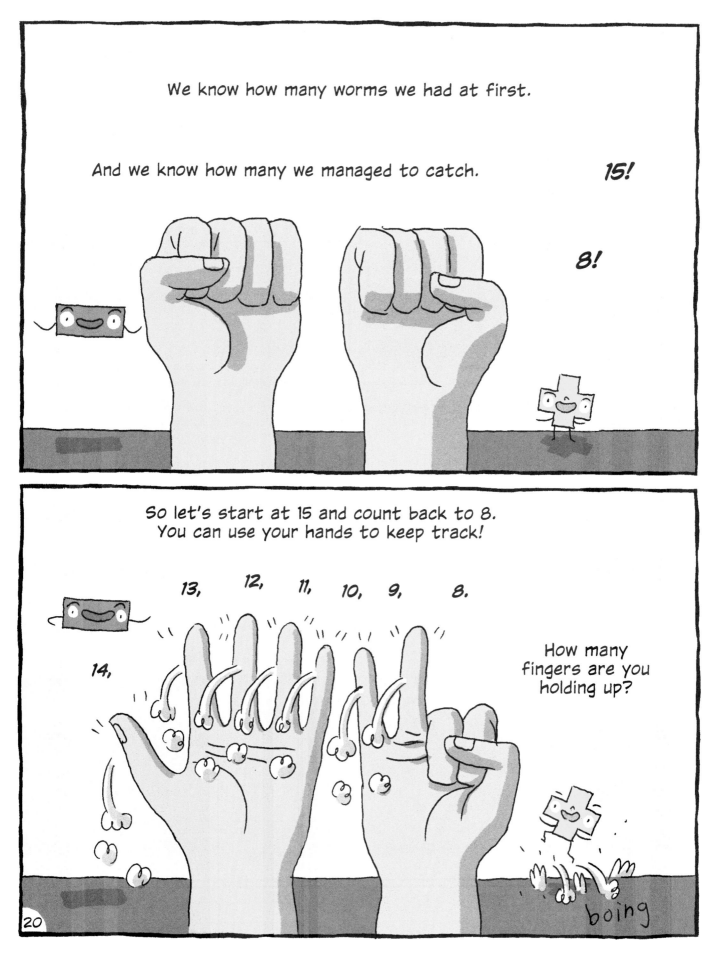

We know how many worms we had at first.

And we know how many we managed to catch.

15!

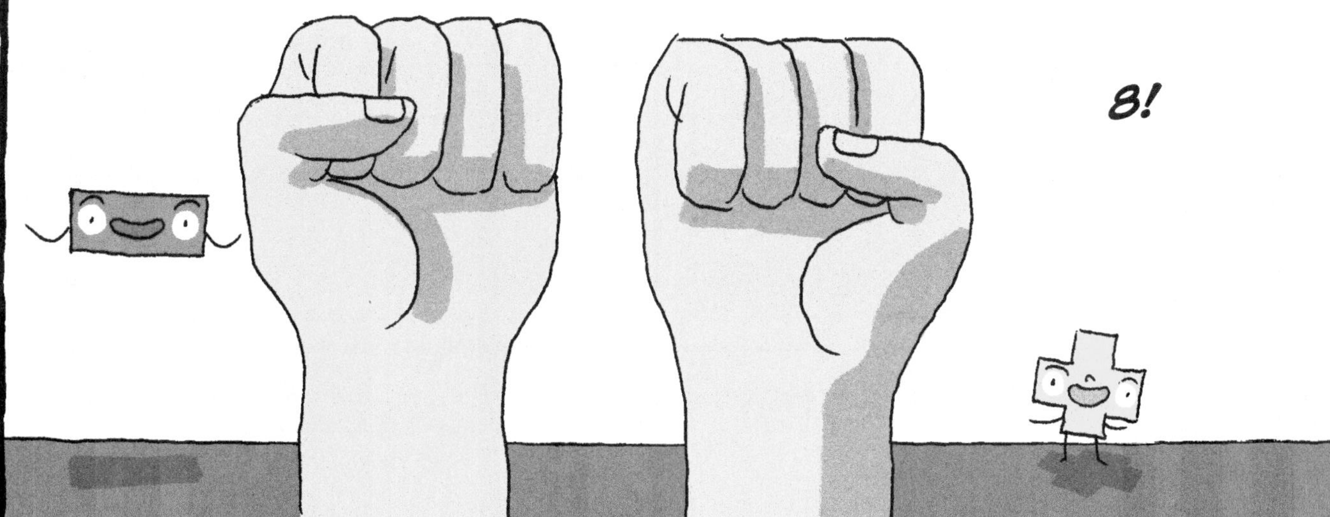

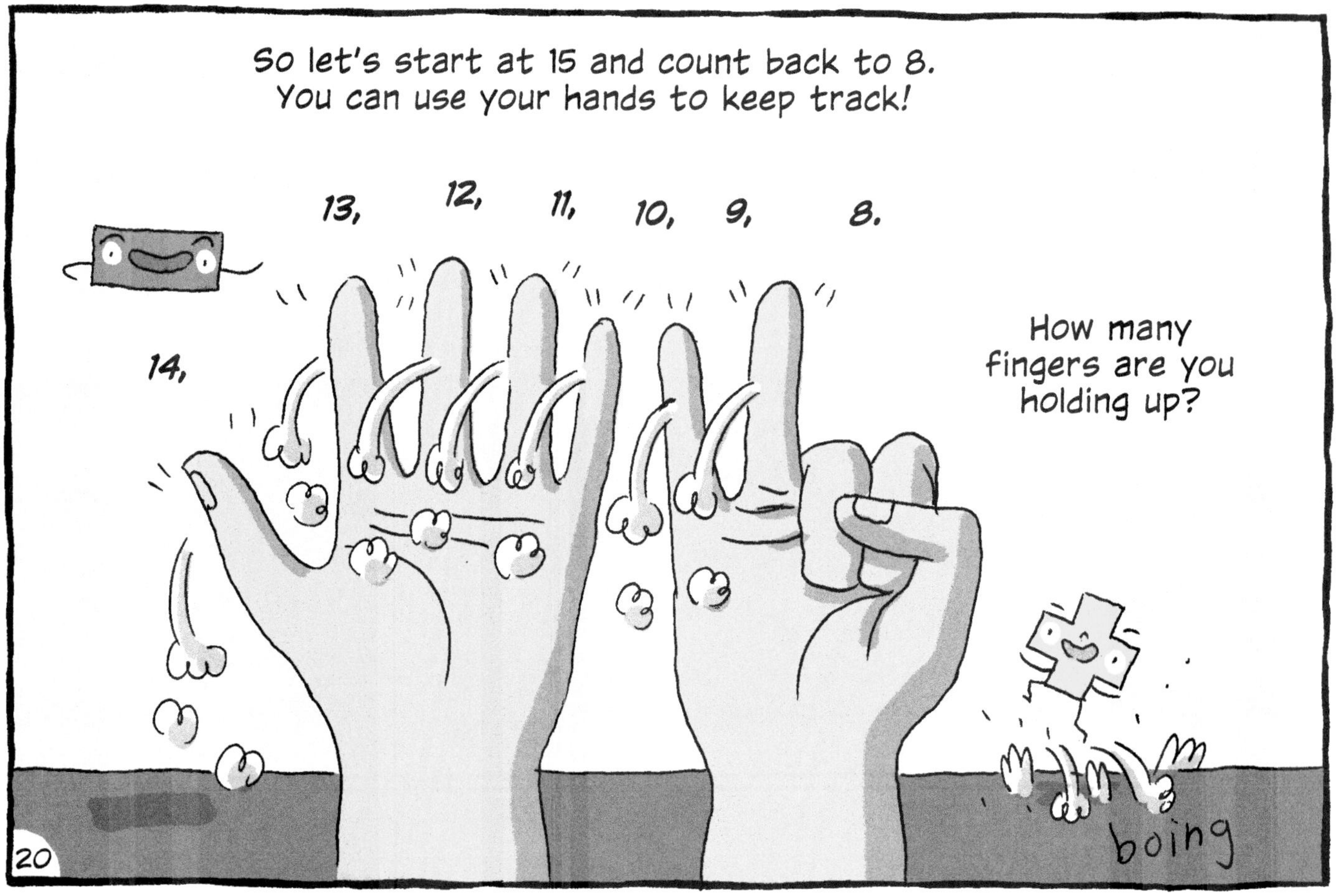

So let's start at 15 and count back to 8.
You can use your hands to keep track!

14, 13, 12, 11, 10, 9, 8.

How many fingers are you holding up?

boing

SEVEN!

That's right!
Seven of us got away!

And we *ain't* coming back!
Nope!

Ha! Ha! Heh! Heh! Ho! Ho! Ha!
Mmm?

Come on. Let's check our work with addition!
Okay!
We can even use a number line!
Burp.

Think of the problem like this:

$$8 + ? = 15$$

Most people find that 10 is easier to work with than 8.

So, let's add 2 to 8 to make 10.

We jumped 2 and
we jumped 5.

2 + 5 = 7

So, we were correct
before. 15 - 7 equals 8!

You got it!

I count 25!

Hey, what are you doing?

Subtracting!

ping

Let's figure it out. There were 25 cars to begin with, and we removed an unknown number...

We need to count up the remaining cars!

So, we can look at the problem like this:

$$25 - ? = 14$$

Why don't we use a number line to help us?

We could start by skip-counting back by 10 to find the answer!

What's 25 - 10?

25

15!

plop

15

25

coal

If we count back
1 more, we have...
14!
15
plop
14

So we jumped back
10 and then 1 more:
10 + 1 =

ELEVEN!
11

Now we know you removed
11 train cars from 25 because
there are 14 train cars left!
That's correct!
chug

You could also
count up from 14 to
find the answer.
Try it!
choo
choo
coal

As different as we are, we sure do work well together!
That's true! No matter how you look at it, the math just adds up!
shake
shake
shake

The best part is, if you find the answer to a problem using one of us...
...you can always use the other one to check your work!

If you come across a math problem
you can't solve, don't give up...

Once you figure it
out, you can show a friend
how to do it, too!

And remember,
if you ever need to
find a difference,
just use me!

I'm
Subtraction!

SUBTRACTION FACTS

This table below can help you add and subtract fast!
It can also help you learn your subtraction fact families.
A fact family shows how groups of numbers are related.

The table shows 10 different fact families for addition and subtraction. Can you think of more fact families?

5 + 5 = 10 10 - 5 = 5	6 + 5 = 11 11 - 5 = 6 11 - 6 = 5	7 + 5 = 12 12 - 5 = 7 12 - 7 = 5	8 + 5 = 13 13 - 5 = 8 13 - 8 = 5	9 + 5 = 14 14 - 5 = 9 14 - 9 = 5
5 + 6 = 11 11 - 6 = 5 11 - 5 = 6	6 + 6 = 12 12 - 6 = 6	7 + 6 = 13 13 - 6 = 7 13 - 7 = 6	8 + 6 = 14 14 - 6 = 8 14 - 8 = 6	9 + 6 = 15 15 - 6 = 9 15 - 9 = 6
5 + 7 = 12 12 - 7 = 5 12 - 5 = 7	6 + 7 = 13 13 - 7 = 6 13 - 6 = 7	7 + 7 = 14 14 - 7 = 7	8 + 7 = 15 15 - 7 = 8 15 - 8 = 7	9 + 7 = 16 16 - 7 = 9 16 - 9 = 7
5 + 8 = 13 13 - 8 = 5 13 - 5 = 8	6 + 8 = 14 14 - 8 = 6 14 - 6 = 8	7 + 8 = 15 15 - 8 = 7 15 - 7 = 8	8 + 8 = 16 16 - 8 = 8	9 + 8 = 17 17 - 8 = 9 17 - 9 = 8
5 + 9 = 14 14 - 9 = 5 14 - 5 = 9	6 + 9 = 15 15 - 9 = 6 15 - 6 = 9	7 + 9 = 16 16 - 9 = 7 16 - 7 = 9	8 + 9 = 17 17 - 9 = 8 17 - 8 = 9	9 + 9 = 18 18 - 9 = 9

FIND OUT MORE

BOOKS

The Action of Subtraction
by Brian Cleary and Brian Gable
(Millbrook Press, 2006)

Help Me Learn Subtraction
by Jean Marzollo
and Chad Phillips
(Holiday House, 2012)

If You Were a Minus Sign
by Trisha Speed Shaskan
and Francesca Carabelli
(Picture Window Books, 2009)

Panda Math: Learning About Subtraction from Hua Mei and Mei Sheng
by Ann Whitehead Nagda
(Henry Holt, 2005)

Pet Store Subtraction
by Simone T. Ribke
(Children's Press, 2007)

Subtracting with Sebastian Pig and Friends: On a Camping Trip
by Jill Anderson
and Amy Huntington
(Enslow Publishers, 2009)

Subtraction at School
by Jennifer Rozines Roy
and Gregory Roy (Marshall
Cavendish Benchmark, 2006)

Subtraction Made Easy
by Rebecca Wingard-Nelson
and Tom LaBaff
(Enslow Elementary, 2005)

What's the Difference? An Endangered Animal Subtraction Story
by Suzanne Slade and Joan C. Waites
(Sylvan Dell Publishing, 2010)

WEBSITES

Cool Math 4 Kids: Subtraction
www.coolmath4kids.com/subtraction/
Lessons, practice activities, and flash cards help kids improve their subtraction skills.

Fun 4 the Brain: Subtraction
www.fun4thebrain.com/subtraction.html
This educational website includes games and printable worksheets that teach the basics of subtraction strategies.

Gamequarium
www.gamequarium.com/subtraction.html
This teacher-designed website provides many pages of games for practice with subtraction, addition, and other math skills.

Kids' Numbers
www.kidsnumbers.com/subtraction.php
Prepare with week-by-week subtraction lessons, and practice your skills with a wide variety of subtraction games.

Math Blaster
www.mathblaster.com/parents/math-games
Math games for all skill sets and all primary grades can be found at this website.

Math Nook: Subtraction Games
www.mathnook.com/math/skill/subtractiongames.php
Fun and challenging games for all ages teach and sharpen subtraction skills.

NOTE TO EDUCATORS

This volume supports a conceptual understanding of subtraction through a series of story problems. As the Subtraction character solves each story problem, it presents different strategies, including variations of direct modeling, counting, and invented strategies. Below is an index of strategies that appear in this volume. For more information about how to use these strategies in the classroom, see the list of Educator Resources at the bottom of this page.

Index of Strategies

Educator Resources

Children's Mathematics: Cognitively Guided Instruction
by Thomas Carpenter, Elizabeth Fennema, Megan L. Franke, Linda Levi, and Susan B. Empson (Heinemann, 1999)

Elementary and Middle School Mathematics: Teaching Developmentally
by John A. Van de Walle, Karen S. Karp, and Jennifer M. Bay-Williams (Harcourt, 2013)

Knowing and Teaching Elementary Mathematics: Teachers' Understanding of Fundamental Mathematics in China and the United States
by Liping Ma (Routledge, 2010)

Young Mathematicians at Work: Constructing Number Sense, Addition, and Subtraction
by Catherine Twomey Fosnot and Maarten Dolk (Heinemann, 2011)